I0149690

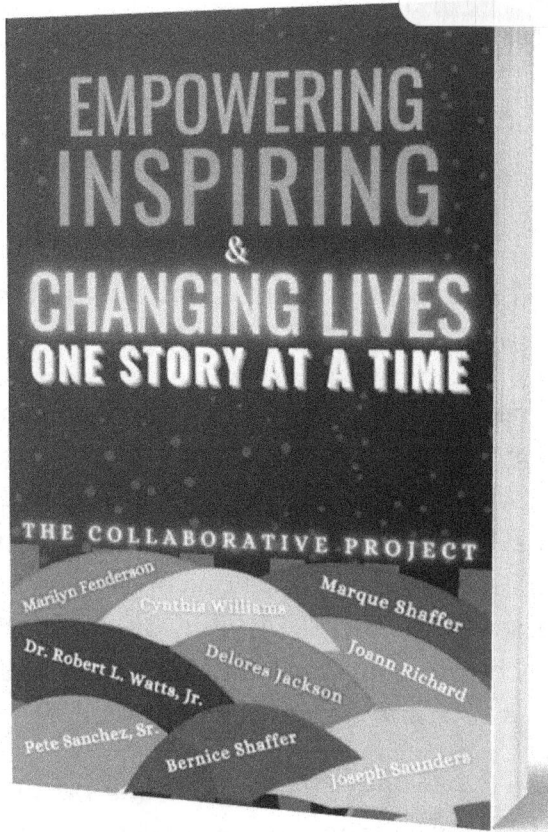

Compiled by

DR. ROBERT L. WATTS, JR.

MARILYN FENDERSON | DELORES JACKSON

JOANN RICHARD | PETE SANCHEZ, SR.

JOSEPH SAUNDERS | BERNICE SHAFFER

MARQUE SHAFFER | CYNTHIA WILLIAMS

EMPOWERING INSPIRING & CHANGING LIVES
ONE STORY AT A TIME

Printed in the United States of America
First Edition, 2021
For information, write to the publisher:
RLW Empowerment Services
P.O. Box 569
Glenwood, IL 60425
info@drrobempowerment.com

"If I can stop one heart from breaking,

I shall not live in vain;

If I can ease one life the aching,

Or cool one pain,

Or help one fainting robin

Unto his nest again,

I shall not live in vain."

by Emily Dickinson (19th Century poet)

CONTENTS

ACKNOWLEDGMENTS

To every family member, friend, that supported and encouraged each of the authors for this book project, we thank each of you. To all those who decided to make the investment and purchase this book, may there be a special transformational blessing in your life and may this book empower you in many ways.

We truly appreciate you.

GOD'S LOVE

LORD, HEAL MY HEART

by

PETE SANCHEZ, SR.

DEDICATION

My darling wife Juanita, I thank you for the continuous encouragement and support to complete this book project and share our testimony of God's grace through our lives. I also want to acknowledge my wonderful children, Leticia, Pete, Jr., Ester Marie, José Orlando; and my grandchildren, Laura, Destiny, Sofia Hope, and Jonathan, Jr. Year after year you all make me so proud of how you show love and support for our family unit. And sending a special thanks to Elders Robert & Natalie Watts for assisting in making this book possible.

We want to give a special thanks to our Senior Pastors, Steve and Melodye Munsey for their mentorship in our lives, since we joined Family Christian Center. We thank them for pouring into our lives as our spiritual leaders and we have grown in a special way because of them.

Pastor Pete Sanchez, Sr. was born in Hammond, Indiana in 1956. He was raised up in the small town of Cotulla, Texas. Then after high school, he met the girl of his dreams, Juanita, and married her on December 4th, 1976. They received Christ as their Lord and Savior in 1977 and have both served Jesus for over 42 years. Currently, Pastor Pete serves as the Spanish Church pastor of Family Christian Center in Munster, Indiana, which is one of the largest and fast-growing churches in America. The Senior pastors are, Dr. Stephen and Pastor Melodye Munsey. Pastor Pete and Elder Juanita gives a special thanks to Dr. Stephen and Pastor Melodye for their trust in the Sanchez Family.

Contact Information:
pastorpetesanchez101@gmail.com

Story One
GOD'S LOVE

I want to share part of my life story with those that are going through painful tragedies and crushed hearts. I come from a family of ten in our family, four sisters and four brothers, my father, and my mother. I married the most beautiful woman on earth, Juanita Garcia Sanchez on December 4, 1976.

One year after, we went through the hardest tragedy of our lives. My younger brother Jose Orlando Sánchez was shot and killed by one of our own friends. I was sick that day and didn't go to work but I wanted to go visit our friends that day, but my wife suggested that I not go, but my brother ended up going over while they were loading up their guns to go and make a drop off to people, they sold to, one of the guns went off and killed him.

Why am I sharing this story? Because I know someone needs to hear what the Lord did for me in my most difficult time and how God showed up to help me in a time of pain and suffering. You and I were not created to walk alone in our struggles and pain. You can't carry that heavy burden alone; we don't have to power nor strength.

The bible says, in 1 Corinthians 16:16, *'Love conquers all things...,'* not that your heart pain will easily go away, but God will love on you so you can make it through each day. Do everything in Love...In John 2:9-10 it says,

Anyone who claims to be in the light and hates his brother or sister is still in darkness, anyone who loves their brother and sister lives in the light and there is nothing in him to make him stumble.

Yes, I had hatred in my heart with the person that killed my brother...But that's when God stepped in to rescue me....my wife became very ill and was in need of surgeries. We were invited to go to a healing revival, and we went. God healed my wife and both of us accepted Jesus Christ as our Savior and were Born-again. We started to go to a little church name Mount Sinai in Hammond, Indiana.

This is where God worked his unfailing Love into our lives The more in His presence, the more we understood how much God loved us. But then one Sunday service, there walks in the friend that shot and killed my brother. I was the music director and guitar player at this church. The presence of God was so strong that at the altar call, that friend came and gave his life to the Lord. Then God began to convict my heart to go and forgive him and I wrestled with it as Jacob wrestled with the angel....'No Lord, I can't!'

God spoke to me saying my son was also killed on the cross for no just reason, and I forgave the hold world, including you. I cried even more, by the time I knew it, I was standing in front of him, and I put my arms around him and forgave him...my life was totally changed still to this day, after 43 years. It's all about understanding how much God loves us. Love will conquer all things...

Proverbs 3:3-4 says, *Let Love and faithfulness never leave you, bind them up around your neck, write them on the tablet of your heart, then you will win favor and a good name in the sight of God and men.*

2 Corinthians 12:10, *Therefore, I take pleasure in infirmities, in destress, in reproach, in persecution for Christ's sake, for when I am weak, then I am strong.* Don't depend on you conquering in your own strength.... God's strength is way stronger than ours.

GOD
LOVES
YOU
SO MUCH!

"For if you forgive other people when they sin against you, your heavenly Father will also forgive you."
Matthew 6:14

Reflections...

_____

_____

_____

_____

_____

_____

_____

_____

SCHOOL IS IN THE HOME

by

JOANN RICHARD

DEDICATION

This writing is dedicated to my son, daughter, and homeschool students. Thank you for our journey of school in the home.

Joann Richard shares her experience as a homeschool parent. She gives you a glimpse into her homeschool journey. Joann found homeschooling to be very rewarding. After her children graduated and entered high school, she continued to homeschool 4 other students at the request of their parents. 3 of the 4 students were high school age. What are the pros and cons of homeschooling? What curriculum does one use? Should a homeschool family join a support group? What resources are available to homeschool families? In "School Is In the Home", Joann answers many of these questions". For the family who believes a home education might be the right choice for their family, school really can be in their home.

Contact Information:
Email: informative12@yahoo.com

Story Two
SCHOOL STARTS AT HOME

*T*here were about 2.5 million homeschooled students throughout the United States in the Spring of 2019. The homeschool population has been growing at an estimated 2% to 8% per year over the past several years.

In 1994, I was a member of the mom and tots' group in my church. I remember it like it was yesterday. That day the guest speaker shared her testimony about what led her to teach her children at home as they reached school age. It was my first-time hearing about homeschooling. It was quite interesting. She had some books for sale about homeschooling for those who were interested. There were many brochures as well as literature about the upcoming annual homeschool convention. At this time, my children were 2 and 3 years of age and I had no intention of homeschooling, yet I listened intently as she shared her experience. I then shared the information that

I had obtained, with a neighbor who was looking for an alternative for schooling her children. She decided to attend the annual homeschool conference that summer and consequently began homeschooling her children.

In August 1995, I enrolled my son Joseph in the pre-kindergarten class. My daughter, Rebecca was enrolled in pre-kindergarten in 1996. I was very pleased with the fact that the school was for pre-kindergarteners ages 3 and 4, kindergarten and 1st-grade students only. The school was equipped with everything you could imagine for students in this age group. I was delighted with my children's progress in school, and they both enjoyed school very much. I was an active parent and attended all school activities as well as the parent-children sessions held at the school every Friday. During the 1997 school year, I presided over the parent-teacher organization for the pre-kindergarten students.

The following year, due to the death of the school superintendent, a new superintendent was assigned. At that time, we began to witness many changes within the school. Some of the changes did not appear to be in the best interest of the students. The school informed us that all teacher assistants would be removed from the classrooms in the upcoming school year. This meant that the number of students the teachers had in their class would go from 15 per assistant and teacher to 30 plus for the teacher.

At the time, there was one assistant or teacher per 15 students. This change was a game-changer for me, as my son Joseph was dyslexic, which would mean less classroom support for him. Joseph completed pre-kindergarten 3, 4 and kindergarten. Rebecca completed prekindergarten 3 and 4, she was a quick learner, filled with joy, and very bubbly.

At the end of the 1998 school year, amidst all the changes, I made the difficult decision to withdraw my children from the school system for the coming school year. In August 1998, it was then that I embarked on the homeschool journey. I began doing extensive research as I prepared to homeschool. I attended the annual homeschool conference and visited many homeschool support groups. I also talked to other families who were already homeschooling. Finally, I opted to join a co-op homeschool group the first year of homeschooling. Our group consisted of 15 families and about 40 children. We met many times throughout the summer to plan subjects, classes, teachers' assignments, and curriculum. Once the school year started, we met twice a week at a local church. The days the support group did not meet, the families and students worked from home. The following school year, I continued with the homeschool co-op group.

In addition to homeschooling, my children were involved in activities within our church, the local library, and day camp during the summers. Joseph was in music lessons and Rebecca was in the girl scouts. I homeschooled Joseph and Rebecca through 8th grade. As we were preparing for Joseph's first year of high school, he surprisingly asked if he could go to high school? We scheduled a meeting with the principal of a private high school of interest. After meeting with the principal, and a family discussion, we enrolled Joseph in high school. I submitted Joseph's application, transcript, and other requested documents to the high school. He was accepted and scheduled for orientation. The following year Rebecca was accepted into the same high school.

Entering Joseph and Rebecca back into school after 9 years of being homeschooled was a smooth transition. I had kept accurate records for attendance, subjects, grades, test scores, and diplomas for our homeschool, Christian Learning Academy. Once back in school, Joseph and Rebecca received numerous compliments from teachers. The most common statement I heard from several teachers is that they could tell Joseph and Rebecca had been homeschooled because they had a desire to learn. I found homeschooling to be very rewarding. After my children were both in high school, I continued to homeschool several students at the request of their parents. I homeschooled 4 students, 3 of whom were high school students.

Perhaps you may have considered the possibility of homeschooling for your family. I want to give you a glimpse into the world of homeschooling. There has been a myriad of new developments and changes in homeschooling over the last few years. There are many different reasons a family might choose a homeschool education for their children. It could be for religious, cultural, financial, health, lifestyle, or other reasons. If you or someone you know is considering embarking on the homeschool journey perhaps the information that I have listed below could be helpful. There are far more options, curriculums, resources, and homeschool groups available today than there were when I first started homeschooling years ago.

SOME PROS OF HOMESCHOOLING

*The opportunity to teach your children your religious beliefs and family values.

*The opportunity to discover and develop your child's unique God-given gifts as part of their education.

*The opportunity to choose a curriculum to compliment your child's learning style. A curriculum that will best meet their needs and develop a love of learning.

While every child can learn, every child's learning style may differ.

Note: Observe your student and ask yourself, what kind of learner is my child? Is he or she a visual learner, Auditory learner, Kinesthetic learner, or reading and writing learner?

*You can better enhance and balance family relationships between children, parents, and siblings.

*Homeschooling is an opportunity to foster a spirit of independence and lifelong learning. Statistics indicate 33% of high school graduates and 42% of college grads never read another book after graduation.

*Homeschooling also provides children with a safe environment from physical violence, bullying, drugs, alcohol, and school shootings. It is quite common today for students to ask to be homeschooled.

*Homeschool children have been known to excel academically and do just as well on standardized test.

*Many Colleges and Universities seek out homeschool students.

SOME CONS OF HOMESCHOOLING

*Some Homeschool families are disorganized. Each family can structure their schooling to meet the needs of their family. School hours, areas of the home for schooling, and a place for school materials must be designated for successful homeschooling. You should create a personalized system that functions for your family.

*Homeschool families not setting up a name for their homeschool. It is vital to select a name for your school. (your school's name is to be used on students' transcripts, documents, graduations diplomas, Identification, and more).

*Homeschool families not focusing on academics. Many distractions will take time away from schooling if a family is not intentional. Limit outside distractions and extracurricular activities during school hours. Learning is the priority.

*Families not keeping updated documentation for their homeschool (attendance, courses, grades, test, and other relevant records).

*Homeschools not teaching student(s) the importance of working within time parameters. Remember, you are preparing your student or students for the world, they should be taught to complete assignments, tests, and skills within an allotted time.

*Homeschool families deciding to go at it alone, without a support group, outside interactions or extracurricular activities. Support is the key.

*Families not asking others to respect the fact they homeschool.

*Advise family members and friend of your hours of operation for your home school. Let them know you are only available after school hours.

*Have a message on your voicemail, as a reminder to callers, you are not available to take calls during the school day.

WHERE DO YOU START?

*The Home School Legal Defense Association HSLDA, https://www.hslda.org. Start here to get many of your questions answered. Learn about the laws for schooling for your state, resources and much more.

*Know the educational requirements of the local school system. This includes required subjects and credits for high school and or college admission.

SUPPORT GROUPS

Local homeschool groups can provide many resources for homeschool families. Our local support group kept our families abreast of many developments and activities to supplement our teaching. These are some of the activities that were accessible to us:

- Gym groups
- Presidential fitness program
- Basketball and other sports
- Science fairs
- Field trips
- Graduations
- Standardized testing
- Spelling contest
- Student Year Books (the students wrote and designed their own yearbook page)
- Homeschool Library (As a resource of homeschool parents)
- Theatre group
- Summer Skate passes
- Reading programs incentives
- Specialized classes
- Volunteer for activities in the community

SPECIALIZED CLASSES

Additional classes were available for students seeking advanced studies.

- Math classes
- Science Classes
- Language Courses
- Advanced level classes

Keep in mind as a tax paying citizen; your student(s) can participate in classes in the local school system (for example our students were able to enroll in the driver's education program in the local school).

Homeschool high school students could also take a college class at the local college at no cost.

*Check your local college. One of our local colleges had a brochure entitled "Opportunities for Homeschooling Families." It offered honor classes and other services.

CURRICULUM CHOICES

*There is no limit to the number and type of curriculums available today.

*Christian Book Distributors has a homeschool catalog (www.cbd.com)(it includes Christian and non-Christian curriculum. This will give you an idea of the many learning resources available.

*Abeka curriculum for Preschool-grade 12. (abeka.com)

*Christian Liberty Academy (christianliberty.com) *Class Homeschools (homeschools.org) (This list is not an exhaustive list; please do your own research).

Today there is a wealth of information available online. In conclusion, for those of you who believe this is the right choice for you, school really can be in your home!

Reflections...

_____

_____

_____

_____

_____

_____

_____

_____

_____

FEAR DON'T LIVE HERE ANYMORE

by

MARILYN FENDERSON

DEDICATION

I would like to dedicate this story to my family members who lost their battle to cancer. To those who have lost loved ones to cancer and to everyone who has battled cancer and won!

Pastor Marilyn Fenderson is an ordained Pastor, Author, Christian Marriage Counseling, Prayer Intercessor and Kingdom Builder. She has authored the books **Tapped For God's Blessing | Spilling The Tea; A Daily Cup of Wisdom | We Put A Ring On It,** which was co-authored with her husband. Her books are currently being sold online locally and globally and are available for purchase at **www.marilynfendersonministries.com/books**, Amazon, Barnes and Noble, React books and various other online bookstores. She has also co-authored several books and written forewords for other authors.

Pastor Marilyn is the founder of Marilyn Fenderson Ministries **www.marilynfendersonministires.com** and along with her husband and ministry partner she is also the co-founder of their marriage ministry One Flesh Worldwide Ministries in 2003 which began as a radio broadcast on WGBX 1570 AM. She has also been inspired to spiritually strengthen and restore marriages through her teachings, writings and revelation knowledge that is demonstrated in her marriage site **www.happywifecontenthusband.com**

Contact Information:

Email: marilynfenderson@yahoo.com
Website: www.marilynfendersonministries.com
Facebook: www.facebook.com/pastormarilynfenderson
Instagram: www.instagram.com/pastormarilynfenderson

Story Three
FEAR DON'T LIVE HERE ANYMORE

*A*t age 50, I heard the words that punched me in my gut and placed my life in a proverbial tailspin, "You have Breast Cancer." Fear, panic, anxiety, and depression attached themselves to the fabric of my soul to make me feel that my life was over. I was afraid to think about my future and what it would look like. I was afraid to tell my family because I wouldn't be able to handle their reaction. I was afraid to let those words settle in my spirit because I couldn't even handle my own reaction. I was completely devastated and overwhelmed with emotion.

My mind became riddled with all types of troubling thoughts. Will I get to see my children get married? Will I get to meet my future grandchildren? What about my dreams? What about all of my plans? I still have things that I need to do, but God said, "slow down, you are getting way ahead of my plan." "It is not by your might or power but by my spirit." "You will not fight this battle, I will." "You will not go through this test alone; I will be there with you." All you need to do is saturate your mind with my word and trust me.

As I hearkened to the voice of the Lord, my spirit was at ease and my mindset shifted. I turned to my doctor with a stern countenance, appearing to be brave but I was sure he could see through my façade. I asked, "what are the next steps? what type of treatment do you recommend? All the while praying in my mind and hoping that it wasn't true. The doctor went on to tell me that he would first need to perform a biopsy to determine if the tumor was benign or malignant. If the results conclude that it is malignant then the next course of action is surgery followed by chemotherapy and radiation treatment.

You can imagine the places that my mind traveled to as I waited impatiently for the results of my biopsy. Whenever the phone would ring, fear would come back and sit right next to me. When I finally received the call, the panic and anxiety came rushing back but I kept praying and meditating on healing scriptures, I was fully persuaded that God had the power to do what he had promised. When I returned to my doctor, he revealed the surgical treatment plan which was to perform a lumpectomy because the tumor was at stage two, so I didn't require a mastectomy. The doctor said, "you are still a young vibrant woman so let's save your 'Ta Tas.' I chuckled and replied, "you got that right Doc, let's do this." At that moment, there was a sense of peace that enveloped my spirit because I knew God was with me.

Prior to my surgery date, I changed my diet to include more leafy green vegetables and I drank alkaline water. I meditated on God's word day and night, and I was very selective about who I shared this news with because I didn't want doubt or worry to set in. I know people mean well but sometimes they tend to say things that just don't resonate in your spirit. For example, "how long do you have? Do you have your affairs in order? They have already put you in the grave when God has put you in peace. I only shared with people of strong faith that were prayer warriors who believed in my healing as much as I did. I was preparing myself for this fight, I was armed with my shield of faith and my feet were fitted with the gospel of peace. God was leading the charge and he was ready for battle.

On the day of the surgery, I was visited by spiritual leaders that prayed for me before my procedure. God was with me, and he sent his soldiers armed with the weapon of prayer. The surgery was a success and the next steps in my treatment were eight weeks of chemo followed by thirty days of radiation. I had to wrap my mind around allowing these chemicals to be injected into my body, so I searched for an alternative treatment. I researched the side effects and how they would impact me which made me fearful all over again. When I spoke to a friend who was also a nurse about the risks of chemo, I asked if she thought a holistic approach was better. She replied" I know a few people who took the holistic approach, and they are not here to talk about it. My eyes popped, well I guess that settles it, chemo, and radiation it is.

As I embarked on my treatment journey, I was scheduled to get chemo infusions once a week for eight weeks. I will never forget my first day in the chemo ward, I was so anxious, nervous, and afraid of what I couldn't control. When I entered the door, there were four other people sitting in chairs with bags of chemicals attached and tubes stuck in their veins. I immediately began to pray and ask God to help me overcome my fear. As I sat down and waited for the chemo to be administered by the nurse, I glanced at the other patients and greeted them with a friendly, 'hello' and a smile.

Some responded and others looked as though they didn't want to be bothered and that was fine, considering what they were going through. As I sat in my chair for an hour receiving the infusions, I could feel the chemicals flowing through my body. In my head, it seemed magnified because I could literally hear it rushing through my veins, but I kept my mind flooded with God's word. Yes, my bible was with me, and reading the word kept me in peace.

In the following weeks, my visits became much easier because my ward mates began to open up and share their stories. I remember thinking, these folks' circumstances are far worse than mine and I began to minister to them about God and how he is a healer. It was at that point that I realized I had found purpose through my pain and peace through my fear. God used me because some of the people were not spiritual at all, but I kept talking about God's goodness and how he would see them through this.

As I continued my treatment, I lost my hair, my eyebrows, and my lashes fell out. All my fingernails and toenails completely fell off and there was numbness in my hands and feet. Although I was suffering through all the effects of the chemo, I persisted in ministering through my afflictions. Those patients needed to see

God's power working through me which increased their faith and understanding of who he is. Pretty soon, I could see the joy in their faces when I entered the chemo ward, they were genuinely happy to see me and eager to hear about God. I remember thinking, God we did it, thank you for using me. On the last day of my treatment, we laughed, we cried, and I prayed with them, fear had been replaced with faith. Afterward, my thirty days of radiation treatments went surprisingly smooth, and I came through it with flying colors. I can now say that I know God to be Jehovah Rapha, the God who heals.

God has not given me a spirit of fear but of love, power, and a sound mind. His love resonates in my soul every day as I practice to love others and see them as God sees them. His power works through me because I am an overcomer and I have conquered my fear which elevates my faith daily. I have a sound mind because God keeps me in perfect peace. My peace transcends all understanding, and the world can't comprehend why I walk in victory.

As I reflect on that day, it has been 12 years and I can say that *fear don't live here anymore.* No weapon that is formed against me will succeed and I have the battle scars to prove it. The enemy's weapons are doubt, discouragement, and fear but God's weapons are hope, courage, and peace. I thought it was a death sentence, but God revealed to me that it was a life sentence. I have learned to be intentional and to live my life on purpose, I walk by faith not sight. I've learned to turn all my troubles over to God because it is he who sustains me. I've learned to love unconditionally and be more forgiving even when wronged by others. I'm looking forward to continuing to live my best life without fear or regrets because I have earned it!

Reflections...

...the devil is a liar!! and the father of all lies!!!
(John 8:44 CEV) then I began to pray!!
If you ask my immediate family members about me, they will
tell you that's one of the first things that will come out of my
mouth, if any negative situation tries to raise its head.

THE POWER OF THE TONGUE

by

BERNICE SHAFFER

DEDICATION

This chapter is dedicated to every believer and, to every unbeliever. To the believers: it's up to you to start making a change in the words you speak out of your mouth, because you will have to give an account for them one day. To the unbeliever: my prayer is that the next words that come out of your mouth, is to ask Jesus to come into your heart and to save you (Romans 10:9,10).

Bernice was born and raised on the south side of Chicago, Illinois (Chi Town) to southern raised parents, Bernice is the third oldest of five siblings. She attended Chicago State University, with a focus on Early Childhood. She also attended Governor State University, where her focus was on music. Bernice knew early in life that her ability to create and write would one day bring her to become a songwriter, producer, and an author. She has written two children's books: *Jasper Williams and the Melting Pot Experience* and *Hello God*. Both books can be purchased on Amazon. Bernice is currently working on another children's book, due for release in 2022.

Amid all the chaos and the pandemic, going on in our world, through much prayer, Bernice was inspired to write and produce her first single, a song of hope to the world: *We Need Each Other*, that was released in March of 2021. The song can be found on all online platforms such as, Spotify, Apple Music, iTunes, Amazon, Pandora, and Deezer.

Contact Information:

Email: bernice@berniceshaffer.com
Website: www.berniceshaffer.com
Instagram: www.instagram.com/shafferparmeley

Story Four

THE POWER OF THE TONGUE

What are you saying? What are you not saying? The day I gave my life to Jesus Christ, was the most wonderful day of my life!! Everything looked the same, but now, my father was no longer satan but GOD!! Oh, happy day! So, now that I am this new Christian, what does this mean? I go to church every Sunday and maybe serve in the church, yea! But soon, I began to learn more by hearing the preacher and reading the Bible. I began reading about the "tongue" and some things I used to say, I knew I could not say any more. I had to change!! I had to watch those things that were coming out of my mouth. I would say whatever came to mind, like; "Boy, that is so dumb," "I'll never get anywhere like this," I'm broke," "I can't do that," "Girl, he's dying to meet you," "I hate you," and even some profanity. You get the picture.

All those negative words were full of doubt and fear.

Unbeknownst to me, I was planting these negative seeds, not only for my life but for my children's lives also. Seeds of negativity, doubt, failure, unbelief, etc. That is how we all talked, that's what we heard. What was so wrong with what I was saying? EVERYTHING WAS WRONG!!! The more I began to read the Bible and hear real preachers teach God's Word, I knew my mouth could never stay the same. God is a God of Faith, not failure, negativity, doubt, or unbelief. The Bible says, "Now without faith, it is impossible to please God, for whoever comes to Him must believe that He exists and that He rewards those who diligently search for Him" (Hebrews 11:6 ISV). The Bible also says, "Death and life are in the power of the tongue, and those who love it will eat its fruit" (Proverbs 18:21 NKJV). What does this mean? Simply, you will have what you keep saying! Those invisible seeds that we don't see with our natural eyes are planted with our words and will sprout up somewhere in your life, good or bad! You will reap what you have sown. So, *what are you saying*?

Why are Words so Important? Our words are so important because we are made in the image of God!! In Genesis 1:26 (KJV), the creation of man begins. And God said, "Let us make man in our image, after our likeness..." What does this mean? We are spiritual beings, who need an earth suit to walk around on this planet until it no longer exists. So, "God created man in His own image, in the image of God, created him; male and female, He created them," (Genesis 1:27 KJV). We have hands, feet, face, eyes, nose, and a mouth to speak like our Father God. "In the beginning, God created the heavens and the earth. The earth was without form and void, and darkness was on the face of the deep..." (Genesis 1:1-2 NKJV).

When God saw the darkness, He DID NOT say; "Oh, my goodness, it's so dark." "What am I going to do?" NO! God spoke out of His mouth what He wanted, He said; "let there be light, and there was light"! God wants us, the believers, to speak what we want, not what we don't want. We must speak the Word of God over any circumstance. Because our words are faith seeds planted all throughout our lives, we must put a watch on our tongue. "You are snared by the words of your mouth; You are taken by the words of your mouth." (Proverbs 6:2 NKJV).

God has given us the authority to speak with our mouths, the authority to speak over any negative situations that will try to raise their heads. As children of the most, high God, He didn't just create us for nothing, no! He made each and every one of us for a purpose, and He expects us to walk in our purpose and callings. We will one day stand before God to answer for our wrong speaking. "But I say to you that for every idle word man may speak, they will give an account of it in the Day of Judgment. For by your words, you will be justified, and by your words, you will be condemned" (Matthew 12:36-37 NKJV). Those scriptures were written in red which means Jesus is speaking! Do we mess up and make mistakes with somethings that we say out of anger, envy, jealousy, malice, or just not thinking, etc.? Yes, we do! But we ask the Lord to forgive us with a sincere heart and keep living our lives in the Lord, allowing Him to change us day by day until the day of His coming.

Be very careful with whom you come into agreement. Someone could have said a negative comment, and then ask you, "Isn't that, right?" or lied about someone and wants you to agree with them in their lie. At that time, you can either come into an agreement with that negativity or say, "I'm sorry, I don't agree with that." The devil has nothing but tricky devices to try and pull you into his trap, don't fall for it!! It's not just what you say, but also what you listen to, allowing garbage to enter into your ear gates. Also, what you watch with your eyes allows negative visions in your mind, and you will keep seeing that negativity over and over. We must guard our ears and eyes.

When I was growing up, I remember hearing," Sticks and stones may break my bones, but words will never hurt me." Well, that certainly is NOT true! Sticks and stones could probably break your bones, but words can *definitely* hurt you! Especially, if they are spoken out of your mouth and are contrary to God's word, bear in mind, your words are planting seeds. Don't forget this scripture, "For by your words, you will be justified, and by your words, you will be condemned," (Matthew 12:37 NKJV). Again, *what are you saying* or *not saying*?

YOU Have Authority!

What do I mean when I say "authority"? As believers, God has given to us authority through Jesus Christ. **"Behold, I give you the authority to trample on serpents and scorpions, and overall, the power of the enemy and nothing shall by any means hurt you"** (Luke 10:19 NKJV*).*

Because you are made in His image, and with the authority given to you, the believer, you speak His word over situations that may occur in your life or around you, but you must BELIEVE and never doubt! The authority that you have is backed by the POWER of God's word! Find the scriptures in the Bible that are befitting to your situation and with the delegated authority given to you, speak over evil, lack, fear, unbelief, etc., whatever it may be, because NOTHING can stand up against God's word! Remember, you *must* Believe and *never* doubt.

My Prayer For You,

Father, in the name of Jesus, I pray that the Holy Spirit will always bring to their remembrance the importance of the words that they speak out of their mouths from this day forward, as they seek you more and more. "I pray that the God of our Lord Jesus Christ, the Father of glory, may give you spiritual wisdom and revelation in your growing knowledge of him" (Ephesians 1:17 IBV). "The eyes of their understanding being enlightened; that you may know what is the hope of His calling, and what the riches of the glory of His inheritance in the saints, and what is the exceeding greatness of His power toward you who believe, according to the working of His mighty power..." Amen.
(Ephesians 1:17-19 NKJV)

Reflections...

_____

_____

_____

_____

_____

_____

_____

_____

A TIME TO DETOX AND PURIFY

Illustrated by Delores Jackson

by

DELORES JACKSON

DEDICATION

A Dedication to My Grandchildren.

May the peace of God be upon your generation.

May God's words bring every heart to salvation.

May you know that all good gifts come from above.

May you know Jesus gave His life, to show you, His love.

May you show your love to Jesus Christ too.

May you show Him by the things you say, and do

I also want to thank Pastor Horace Smith and Pastor James Meeks, for the way you both teach and explain Black History. It is appreciated.

Delores Jackson, born in the city of West Point, Mississippi. At the age of two, she and her family moved north to Gary, Indiana. She's a graduate from Calumet High School. Delores continued her education studies through Calumet College. (Biblical studies), Harvest-In-Time Christian University (Gary, Indiana Campus), Cross College (Munster, Indiana). She finished her Biblical studies through The Ministerial Alliance, State of Illinois. She is a free- lance artist, illustrator, author of children's books, doll collector, seamstress, t-shirt designer. She is the founder of God's Shining Little Stars Preschool. Now she is a retired preschool teacher, former Sunday school teacher, and former Children's Church Leader, alongside her husband, Marlowe Jackson Sr. of 44 years.

She is an ordain Elder and serving in the ministries of Marriage, Baptism, and Children, alongside her husband. They have three wonderful adult children, a daughter, Shenette, and twin sons, Marlowe Jr. (Brittany) and Marco. They have been blessed with three precious grandchildren, Miguel, Dallis, and Kameron. She gives all praises and glory to God. He has blessed her life with so much love and compassion to share with the world.

Contact Information:

Email: babydoll080953@aol.com

Facebook: www.facebook.com/delores.jackson.984

Story Five
A TIME TO DETOX AND PURIFY

What is Detox? The Dictionary defines detox as: A process or period of time in which one abstains from or rids the body of toxic or unhealthy substances, detoxication.

What is purify? One Dictionary states: 1. Remove contaminants from. 2.To extract something from. Houghton Mifflin Dictionary states: To make pure, to cleanse.

Now we understand, if we need to detox or to purify, that means, there is something clogging up and stopping other things from flowing through freely. It is time for us to get rid all the evil (bad) things in our lives and replace them with righteous (good) things instead. These things maybe, bad habits, bad thoughts, and bad behaviors. Yes, you are right. We all have some of these things in our lives. Some of us are dealing with them ALL! The first step to detoxing and purifying is to renew our mind. There are three important things we need to do, they are:

1. Read the word of God
2. Apply the word of God
3. Live by the word of God

Romans 12:2

"Be not conform any longer to the pattern of this world but, be transformed by the renewing of your mind. Then you will be able to test and approve what God's will is – his good, pleasing and perfect will."

Now, we want to check and examine ourselves. Ready, make a list what you are negative about and what does God's words say about it.

In examining ourselves we must know:

Ephesians 6:12

"For we wrestle not against flesh and blood, but against principalities, against powers, against the rulers of the darkness of this world, against spiritual wickedness in high place."

So now you know where all the bad habits, bad behaviors, bad attitudes, and all sins are formed and from the wicked one, the devil. It is his spirit that enters people, and situations to cause chaos! Let's DETOX!

I know you are saying to yourselves, "but, I do a lot of good things!".

James 1:17

"Every good and perfect gift is from above, and cometh down from the Father of lights, with whom is no variableness, neither shadow of turning"

Wow! Let's thank the Lord for all the good and righteousness that He has put in us. He is such a wonderful Father and Shepherd that He loves us in spite of ourselves! Thank You Jesus, for loving all of us. Yes, our Heavenly Father loves all Races of people! Romans 2:11 "For there is no respect of persons with God."

John 3:16, "For God so loved the world, that he gave his only begotten Son, that whosoever believeth in him should not perish, but have everlasting life."

I want to share a story with you 'I was born in West Point; Mississippi 1952. My parents moved the family, themselves and five children to Gary, Indiana, when I was only two years old. My mother, a Christian woman, had an eighth-grade education. This was very grand for Black People, in those days, in the South. I was told, her dad, my grandfather, did well. He left a house for each of his children and a store when he died. I understand from my mother, in his lifetime, he pretended to be illiterate, because in those days, Black People, dared not let White people know that they were intelligent, could read or write. So, my mother came from a more middle-class Black family. She spoke English very well and expected us to do so as well. My dad's life was totally different. He was on the tail end of slavery life. His mother died giving birth to him. He would have grown up in that slavery lifestyle, had it not been for the love and kindness of his older sister. She took him and helped raised him. Thank you, Lord for her kindness. My dad had no education. He couldn't read or write. He was very intelligent, talented, an artist, hard and faithful worker. He would create his own system of how to do everything. I understand when my dad began courting my mom, he told her that, he had a bank account and a good job. I was told my dad told all those lies so he could marry my mother. Her dad, my grandfather didn't approve of my dad courting his daughter. He wanted better for her. So, my dad lied so he could marry the lady he loved, my mother. Mother told me after a while, she never saw any extra money. The only money they had was from odd jobs, my dad did. So, she confronted my dad, and he confessed his love for her, was his reason for his lying.

In our home growing up there were no racial prejudice. All we were taught a person was BAD or GOOD!

Every race was welcome in our home if they were respectful. They ate my mother's good cooking. Sometimes they brought some of their good cooking. We met many different races, because of my dad's job and he was a great outdoor sports man. He did lots of fishing and hunting. So, his traveled on many weekends. He had by then found a good laboring job, at a foundry in Griffin, Indiana.

All was going well for a few years until a law came out. Every man had to write their name and NOT Just MAKE a X anymore. If they could not write their name, by a certain deadline, NO Job! My dad turns to my wonderful sister. Who was ten years older than I. She began to teach him. His pride would get in the way, and he would yell and say mean things to her. She would just cry. He took quite a while for him to learn to write his name. He did learn in time for the deadline. He was able to keep his job! Thank You, Lord, and my sister!

I attend all Black schools until 7th grade. I received a letter that stated, I was chosen to attend Baily Jr High School. One of the second groups of Blacks to segregate Baily Jr. High School. I was an honor student before I got there and an honor student there, as well. I loved the school, my teachers, and the students. It was my ideal school! Then graduation from Jr. High to high school. Lew Wallace High, another good school, I loved. In 9th grade, good grades, but not in History, not my best subject. I wasn't good at history dates and locations. The teacher needed some help in her life, in many ways. I assume she wasn't used to teaching, Black History, because what she did was JUST WRONG! She showed a film in class about Africa. The Africans were wearing very little clothing. Almost nothing. Their bodies shaking and dangling as they danced. You would have thought she would turn the film off when she saw the lack of clothing. She didn't. There were only three Black girls and one Black boy in class. The rest were all White students. What a hurt and so much laugher from SOME of the White students. Some White students were hurt, angry and upset as we, the Black students were. Shame on that teacher!! My first experience in feeling a Difference! How could a woman do this to 9th graders? Especially the upper part of women's bodies in front of BOYS! Wickedness and evil have no respectful of person. It will get into a BODY or MIND of anyone and cause them to do wrong. The wicked one will do evil things to itself as well as to others. It will cause you to go to Hell instead of Heaven. We must turn from our wicked ways and pray. I hope Mrs. R. that History teacher's life is right with the Lord now. I must say many White parents took care of that situation. Thank you, Lord!

Another incident happened that year, in my swimming class. I did well and earn the credits to go from level to level. It was time for me to go to the deep level of the pool! The teacher Mrs. C. instructed me to get in the water and I did! I wasn't ready to swim in the deep level. I was sinking and sinking fast! All I could hear my teacher Yelling," GET THE Pole! GET THE Pole!" I couldn't see a pole. I began to pray, "I told God I was coming to be with Him". In a few seconds I heard Splash! And another Splash! Two classmates had dived into the water, with their strength and their friendship to save me! They brought me out of that water. This very day I still call them "Goodness and Mercy." Like the prayer says, "Goodness and Mercy shall follow me all the days of my life and I will dwell in the house of the Lord forever." Again, I say, "Thank You Lord! For Your Goodness and Your Mercy." That teacher never took her shoes off or anything to dive in and save me. She was going to let me drown! She didn't check on me even after

I got out of the water. I pray her life is right with the Lord.

That summer my dad took ill. We lost our home, nice neighbors, and the school I loved. We moved to a place called The Small Farm, where I was treated so very badly by many Black students. I was raped by a one-eyed young man. Who was so sorry he had raped a virgin because blood was everywhere! He was believing gossip; lies, he had heard about me. Yes, The New pretty girl. The wicked, jealous spirits in people, spreading lies and people listening and obeying the evil ones. The evil had spread lies to not only steal my virginity but, to kill and destroy my spirit and soul. That young man didn't know the wicked one was after his soul as well. It was a terrible place for an attractive, talented, fashion- model (Sears and Penney's as a child), and an honor student. I was a teenager with a sick dad, a sad new location, not a house but an old apartment building. "Lord, please protect me from this nightmare!" I prayed.

God was so faithful to his word. I pretend to like that rapist to keep him in sight in case I was pregnant or ended up with any disease. When my menstrual came. I was so grateful to God. I told that one eyed man, never ever come around me again. If he ever did, I would surely report him. Later, I found out, he had raped many girls in that area. I hope he got is soul right with The Lord. That January, a very cold day, I went to my locker to get my books for my next class and pieces of material came flying out at me like feathers! Two students got into my locker and shredded my coat into those pieces. A boy because I would not date him. The girl did it out of jealousy. Wow! I forgive everyone that has mistreated, and lied on me, and you must also forgive. I shared some of the bad situations in that location. So now let me share God's goodness with you. The teachers I had were nice. My English teacher, no one greater than, The One and The Only Miss Johnnie McCray!! What a teacher! I had good friends like Jesse, Judy, Rose, Leonia, Maxine, Milly, a real gentleman, Jeffrey, and last but not lest my precious husband. They all attend Calumet High School. God is so Good! Good news, there were some good people, of all races, at Calumet High School also. That area just had never met a person like me before. So many of them kept telling me, that I was so different. I give all praises to God for creating and designing me for His purpose. My life has been a combination of Joseph, the jealousy and abandonment by siblings, Heavenly Father gave me the multicolor coat (anointing) Ester, God created and designed her beauty and graciousness and Job, no matter what happened to Job, he loved God. I belong to God. The one who created me! YOU! belong to God Also. "He made you and not you, yourself." He has great plans for you in spite of all the traps and schemes of the devil and his cohorts. Let's detox all evil out daily and cleanse our mind, hearts, and spirit with more of God's word daily!

➢ The one-eyed young man, who stole my virginity---Black

- ➤ The two that shredded my coat---(Boy) Black and (Girl) White

- ➤ The teacher that made shamed me in History Class---White

- ➤ The swimming teacher that was going to let me drown---Black

- ➤ The classmates that saved my life---Both White

- ➤ The outstanding English teacher---Black

I shared this little list to say, "It is time to detox and cleanse our heart, mind, and live the life God created for us. Live in His peace. Let's be so busy acting like Jesus and looking for Jesus' character in everyone. Let's practice treating people according to their character and stop treating them according to their skin. I know it's hard to do. Let's practice until we get it right. So, God can look down and be proud of us all. Don't let the devil rule you on earth because he wants your soul to burn with him, the devil. Choose God's peace on earth and have eternal life in Glory.

John 3:16

"For God so loved the world that he gave his only begotten Son. That who soever believe in him shall not perish but have eternal life."

Phippians4:6-7

"Do Not Worry About Anything. Instead Pray About Everything. Do not worry about anything, instead pray about everything. Tell God what you need and thank him for all he has done."

Philippians 4: 8,9

"Finally, brothers, whatever is true, whatever is noble, whatever, is right, whatever is pure, whatever is lovely, whatever is admirable-if anything is excellent or praiseworthy-think about such things. Whatever you have learned or received or heard from me or seen in me-put it into practice. And the God of peace will be with you."

Philippians 4:7

"And the peace of God, which surpasses all understanding, will guard your hearts and minds through Christ Jesus."

Proverbs 12:22-24

"The Lord hates lying lips, but those who speak the truth are His joy." A wiseman hides how much learning he has, but the heart of fools makes known their foolish ways.

The hand of those who do their best will rule, but the lazy hand will be made to work."

I shared these things with so you may start detoxing and cleanse your mind and heart from allowing the enemy to tell you lies about a person because of the color of their skin. I hope you will not let the devil use you to say or do wicked things to people and lose your soul. Let's cleanse and detox all evil from our families. Let's Practice and practice, each home, each community. Let's look for the spirit and the attitude in a person first. No one wants to be around disrespectful people, no matter the color of their skin or race. Amen.

This Detox and Cleansing started with one question that was asked by a longtime friend. She was not trying to be rude or anything. She just wanted to know. "Why do Black People behave so badly now, when slavery was such a long time ago?" I stopped and thought a minute. I wanted to hear from the Holy Spirit first. I wanted to be careful of the words that would come out of my mouth. This is what came out, "Some Black People, behave in such a bad way sometimes, because Some White People won't and don't let them forget that they are people of color, and their background was slavery." Some White People remind the Black People that they are Black. when they go to school, when they apply for jobs, when they go out to eat, when they apply for a home, when they apply for college, when they are driving their car, when they are walking in the park, Oh yes, even in the church! Many White People pack up their families and leave the churches. Black People know that they are people of color, and their background and past was slavery. Their lifeline, history, family memories, and their inheritance, dreams, and their plans for their future all destroyed for generations, and generations! The Wicked ones stole them from their land and taught them to hate one other, fight one another, tell on one another, whip and to kill one another. Yes, they were commanded to be hurt or be killed if they didn't obey. Now, is the time to Stop this wickedness by telling the truth The Blacks are the only race that was stolen, mistreated, and brought to America. Tell the truth They have done well in spite of all the evil that has been rooted in them.

The wicked evil ones that did the crime and caused all this pain and hurt to the Africans and America.

They broke every one of the Ten Commandments that God gave Moses and started the division where there should and could have been PEACE!

Commandments:

1. "I am the Lord thy God; thou shall not have any gods before me."
    (The wicked ones demanded to be called Masters, and treated like god)

2. "Thou shall not take the name of the Lord thy God in vain."

   (The wicked ones used cursing words to and over the slaves)

3. "Remember to keep holy the Sabbath Day"

   (The slaves were mistreated every day!)

4. "Honor thy father and thy mother"

   (The slaves that were parents, were taken from their children. The slave children were taken from their parents, so they couldn't honor anyone but the slave owners, the masters.)

5. "Thou shall not Kill."

   (The wicked ones not only killed the slave's bodies, but their identity, strength, spirit, love, joy, peace,

   gentleness, faith, meekness but they did experience longsuffering. The fruit of the spirit was killed out of them. Gal.5:22)

6. "Thou shall not commit adultery"

   (The wicked one raped the slaves, men and women, whether the slaves were married or not, it didn't matter. Evil is Evil! They made slaves rape one another even

their own children and relatives.)

7.   "Thou shall not steal"

(These wicked ones entered a land that was not theirs, it belongs to God. They stole people, who belong to God. The Africans were of all ages, and all circumstances. Some were to be queens, kings, doctors, some were pregnant, little children, teachers, some were to be married the next day. Can you imagine your whole life being taken from you, to be a Slave!)

8.   "Thou shall not bear false witness"

(The wicked ones would tell lies on the slaves. They would accuse the slaves of raping them or their daughters. They would accuse slaves of stealing. The slaves were punished or worse. Guilty or Not!)

9.   "Thou shall not covet thy neighbor's wife."

(Many slaves that were wives were taken from their husbands. Some were raped right in front of their husbands. The husbands could not say a word, because if they did they would be whipped or killed.)

10.   "Thou shall not covet thy neighbor's goods"

(Africans were taken from Africa, not to be helped, not to be educated, not to be given a paying job, but like a thief, the wicked evil ones came to steal, kill, and destroy God's people. John10:10)

I want you to know many precious White people lost their lives, because they didn't agree with the cruel things that was being done to those living human beings. Many Whites suffered because, they were caught being kind to slaves or teaching them to read or write. Many Whites and Slaves became good friends but had to keep it a secret. Some Whites and some slaves truly fell in love with one another. That was truly a No! No! Whites may mistreat Blacks is okay, but to be kind to them was against their law.

So, God's people it is time to Detox and Cleanse our minds and hearts of all the lies we have been led to believe. Let's think, you can only imagine," How the White race would have felt if it had been them instead of Blacks?" Something to think about. Even a free animal is different than a caged and mistreated one.

John 3:16 "For God so loved the world that he gave his only begotten son, that who soever believed in him shall not perish but have everlasting life." Let's love each other so we can have eternal life and when we leave earth let Our Heavenly Father say to all of us, "Well Done My Good and Faithful Servant!"

Attention: The Black families please detox and cleanse every slavery spirit out of you and your family, cursing words are the devil's vocabulary, hitting and fighting one another, disrespecting one another, males don't want to go to school and learn, so they can get a job, having sex without honoring marriage, making homes safe and better for the family, little or no respect for God, Our heavenly Father or His Son, Jesus Christ, shooting, killing, stealing, no more raping , having sex with children , you are not a slave anymore, men not knowing how to treat a woman, low self-esteem, showing body parts in public, speaking broken English thinking it's alright and soulful, thinking everything that is out of order, the person is acting Black. If the person is clean, neat, speak correct English, and like God's best, that person is acting White. Time to Detox and Cleanse, Remember you are not a slave anymore. You are free to read, write and dreams to come true doing it God's way. help our families live heaven on earth!

Attention: The White families please detox and cleanse every slave owner spirit out of you and your family, cursing words are the devils, hitting and fighting one another. Disrespecting others, treating people according to their skin color, only wanting to steal ideas and make money from other's ideas and talents, making others feel less than, because they aren't your race, only wanting to be around attractive people, when you aren't all that cute. Remember everyone is beautiful to God. Ask God to forgive all those that stole, killed, and destroyed all those lives. You are not anyone's master. God is the only Master and Creator, No one works for free, pay and be respectful and fair. Leadership does not mean to disrespect followers, and helpers. Let's all pray for every one of God's children all around the world.

I still wonder in my heart what would have happened to that evil spirit in that policeman, if George Floyd had called the name of Jesus instead of calling his mother! Just imagine!

The friend that asked the question about the behavior of some Black People, said no one ever told her how Black People really got to America. Many people, young and old don't know the truth. Let's pray.

Matthew 6:9-13 (KJV)
"After this manner therefore pray ye. Our Father which art in heaven, Hallowed be thy name. Thy kingdom come. Thy will be done on earth as it is in heaven, Give us this day our daily bread. And forgive our debts as we forgive our debtors. And lead us not into temptation but deliver us from evil. For thine is the kingdom, and the power and the glory forever. Amen."

I close with this statement:

''MORE COMMUNICATION. LESS FRUSTRATION!''
by Delores Jackson

And this song. Please find it and listen.
"Let There Be Peace on Earth, and Let it begin with ME!
"By Jill Jackson Miller and Sy Miller

Love and Blessings,

Delores Jackson

Reflections...

THE PATH OF THE UPRIGHT

by

JOSEPH SAUNDERS
aka
JUSTUS

DEDICATION

I dedicate this to my family that has stood with me through the hardest times of my life & that has molded me into the Man that I now am. I am forever grateful & thankful.

Joseph a.k.a. Justus was born & raised on Chicago's south side. Growing up Joseph survived Life's experiences of Gangs Violence & drugs & eventually turned his life around to whereas now he is a Youth Mentor, Life Skills instructor, Rapper/Poet & Activist in communities across the Chicago area. Justus has traveled extensively throughout the U.S., Thailand & Australia where he promotes Justice through the form of rap. One thing Justus says he wants to be remembered for is that he Loved The People and that he gave his all to serve them.

Contact Information:

Email: humblenessb4honor@yahoo.com
Facebook: www.facebook.com/josefcorleone777
Instagram: www.instagram.com/justus4mypeople/

Story Six

THE PATH OF THE UPRIGHT

*B*ack in the day the only true love I had were for my fam
& some friends/
Even then my definition of love was distorted, fractured,
broken in/
Having pieces of a puzzle that would never end.

Started young in promiscuity/
Just seemed like that was the way to be/
Careless bout her & how I abused her mind, Soul & body/
Seemed to me Money was the true love connection/
For sure my keen attention towards many
Women wasn't showing me any progression.

Many promises & professions I made unto the Lord
would just be broken/
Getting by like life's a token.

Sitting there joking smoking weed like there's no tomorrow/ In my pain & sorrows/
Monday thru Friday would be/
Quenched by Saturdays Hennessy/
While my ladies lay by my side doing the same thing tomorrow night.

Things would never change how it seemed to me/
As long as I had my weed, a 40, & some shorties
Life was good as could be/
Parties night after night , Fight after fight was getting tired in my sight/
I knew this wasn't right.

Knew I wasn't supposed to be living like this.
Blaze up and-relax a bit/
"Don't get into no devilment!"-Grandma steadily told me/
"Well grandma, what other life is there to live?" Couldn't nobody show me.

All I could see was evil around me/
TV only increased negativity/
Producing a mean mentality/
Left my job because Bob had some supreme authority.

As for me I'd given up on life/
It served me no purpose.
Staying up till dusk plotting on ways to earn some bucks just enough for a sack then back to the same ole same ole
Look I gotta go/
Get away from this life come closer to the real me/

Don't really know where to go but to follow the path
righteously.

II.

I didn't know God, but he sure knew me/
Thought I knew love/
Yet he showed me loves real reality/
"Come follow me" a voice in my head said/
Nah that can't be…

"Come follow," says that soft voice hollow./
"Not today maybe tomorrow."/
"Today's thrill may lead to tomorrow's ruin."/
Devil just misconstruing my decision….

Lord just give me Wisdom to know what's right…which
way to move./
"Follow me & Path corrupted will be made smooth."/
"Show & prove!" Was not my attitude… just believe,
have faith./
Best things come to those who wait.

For goodness' sake I was willing to take some of my
precious time/
Give it to God/
Make some use of it./
That seemed fine.

One day decision & I found myself in a stadium full of
men/
White, black, Hispanic/

That's ironic/
I'm feeling kinda good and high but not off that chronic.

I've finally found the hidden tonic that was missing for
so long/
Lord forgive me for my sins I know I've done wrong/
Repent! Turn your life around was what was preached/
That day I was reached

And I took the Lord's hands/
Sincerely gave my life to Jesus and new things began/
Shook and hugged the hand and soul of a white man/

Which showed me love had no color or ending/
Spending quality time with the Lord in love with
wisdom/
These words I speak, may they be imbedded in your
heart & rooted in God's kingdom.

III.

The route usually not taken/
God showed me and promised that I would not be
forsaken/
Making moves with God meant giving up time/
Fine females, smoking and drinking, a hobby of mine.

Had to be pushed behind/
Found out you can't intertwine old ways with what God
had in mind/
For He's seen way before you saw/
Will get in touch with you before you decide to call/

Unto the lord, glory be his name/
Once you meet him don't expect to be the same/
You see… fame I'll catch down here, but my fortune is up there/
A fare must be paid/
For the crown of glory to be laid.

Upon your head stay firm/
Don't switch to tails/
For hell calls out for my name, but my purpose will remain the same!

To shame the devil forever/
Never-will I stop till the Lord takes me up top/
Upon this rock his temple stands firm/
Concerned I use to be on how my life would end/
Not knowing it already had….
Now the new….
Must begin.

Reflections...

WHAT DID MY FATHER SAY?

by

CYNTHIA WILLIAMS

DEDICATION

I dedicate this to the most amazing DAD a girl could be gifted with James Franklin Banks. Rest well in Heaven and Thank you for always loving me.

To my family who has traveled with me on this journey of life and for encouraging me to write and share a part of my story. And I dedicate this to me to never take your foot off the gas.

The question that should always be in the forefront is, What did my dad say?

Cynthia Williams is a loving wife of Kenneth for over 30 years and the proud mother of Nick, Chris, Kendra, and Kennadie aka mother's baby. She is also a realtor with Competence, Confidence, Charisma and Class who places a priority on providing exceptional customer service to her clients for all their housing needs. Cynthia started her housing career in 1990 working for the U.S. Department of Housing & Urban Development (HUD), where she gained first-hand experience with first time homebuyers, realtors, Section 8, defaults, foreclosures, credit counseling for homebuyer, fair housing rules and regulations, FHA requirements, approvals, and mortgage qualifications. During her tenure Cynthia was nominated by her peers and received The Secretary's Outstanding Achievement Award, the highest Award given by the Secretary to exceptional government employees.

Cynthia is a natural when it comes to engaging and understanding the needs and desires of her clients. With a contagious laugh and outgoing personality, she became a beacon of light to her clients who needed special attention. Her common sense approach provides all her clients the security and comfort needed for an easy buying or selling process.

As a proud resident of northwest Indiana, she takes pride in her contribution to the community. Cynthia is a spokesperson for the American Heart Association, a mentor and leader at the Family Christian Center and a committed volunteer at G.A.P. Food Pantry in Crown Point. Cynthia is also a graduate of the IAR Leadership Academy and recipient of the Thea Bowman Humanitarian award. She is a PTO volunteer, Girl Scout troop leader and an ordained pastor.

Contact Information:

Email: pastorc69@gmail.com
Facebook: www.facebook.com/profile.php?id=725468283

Story Seven
WHAT DID MY FATHER SAY?

*A*s a young girl, I remember many things. I remember 105th and calumet the street I grew up on, I remember my Kindergarten teacher Ms. Shields, I remember playing double Dutch outside with my sisters and the girls off the block, I remember the first time I rode the yellow bike that my brother gave me and my sister for Christmas, We could not wait to ride our bikes and we did right there in the snow we did not care how cold it was or how slippery it was we just wanted to ride our new yellow bikes. My brother was on one side to start us off and my dad on the other side to catch us and to make sure we didn't go too far.

I remember learning how to drive in the alley of 105th and calumet and my dad making sure I didn't run into the garbage cans and our neighbor's garage. I thought it was strange that my dad would teach me how to drive a car in an alley later he told me it was to teach me the discipline to stay in my own lane. I remember my first car my dad bought me for graduation, a brown 1983 duster with cream shaggy wool seat covers. I loved that car and loved my dad even the more for getting me the perfect gift.

I remember walking to school on concrete pavement and playing hopscotch on the way and thinking I was a big girl because my dad let me walk to school with my friends. I remember running home to beat the streetlights so my dad would not put me on punishment. I remember my dad sitting in the kitchen with me and my sisters as my mom would press our hair bone straight and he would tell us, don't cry it's almost over, and would ask the question don't you want to look pretty for daddy?

I remember my dad teaching me how to drive a stick shift car the day we took it off the lot. I never had driven one before, so he literally taught me how to drive the car on the car lot we purchased it from. I drove it for a couple of minutes as my dad watched and then my dad said, "OK, now it's time to go home." I thought to myself I'm not ready, I need more practice, and why is he doing this to me, but my dad saw the ability in me that I didn't even see in myself. Sometimes and oftentimes in life, we try to wait for the perfect opportunity to come along, we wait until after the rehearsals are done after all the practices are completed to pick the perfect time for our own readiness, and most of the time we are still not ready.

I remember being terrified driving a stick shift car home by myself, but my dad drove behind me and said you can do this! Now I knew how to drive a car, but a stick shift was out of my league. I remember having to go up a hill and I panicked because the car started rolling backward and I grabbed the emergency brake and the car shut off in the middle of the street. My dad and several other cars were behind me and I couldn't move because fear had gripped me so bad and made me think the car was going to flip over, or I was going to cause this major car accident and kill myself and the people behind me. So, I just sat there crying while the horns were honking. I could hear my dad telling me to go but I just was too scared.

After what seemed like hours, which probably was only about 2-3 minutes, I could see my dad getting out of our old dusty reliable station wagon exchanging words with the cars behind us and waving them around, and leaning into the window saying, 'What's wrong? And why did you stop?' I told him I started rolling backward and I got scared and panicked. My dad told me I had to release the clutch (the thing that is holding the car in gear) and give it some gas (momentum) at the same time to keep it from going backward. It amazes me how a little lesson in driving a car and words from my dad would be the platform for a successful life. As I reflect over the many things that have happened in my life, things that I just couldn't seem to let go of, and things that would not let go of me. I can hear my dad say, 'RELEASE AND GIVE IT SOME GAS!'

Things that have a clutch on me or I've had a clutch on, has paralyzed me or caused me to stay in one position because of fear of the outcome. What if I roll backward or would I just stay neutral in this situation, when all I had to do was release the hook or the clutch and get my momentum back. Little did my father know those simple words from him to help me drive a vehicle that I've never driven would be the words of a game changer!

I desperately wanted my dad to drive the car up the hill so I could just go home, and he said no, but I got your back and their ain't nothing you can't do without a little gas. So, I tried it. The first time the car started rolling back and I turned it off. The second time same thing. I tried it multiple times and did the same thing. I could hear my dad saying do it at the same time and you will get up and over the hill. I Just could not imagine releasing one thing to go forward with another thing, little did I know then that is exactly what I needed to do all along. As we go in life it is the little things that we need to release in order to go forward, and it is the little things that get you stuck. It is the little things that cause the biggest holdup, and the simplest thing that we can do is to release our clutches.

My father was many things, a protector, a provider, a cook, a shoulder to lean on, a truant officer to me and my siblings, a strong yet gentle disciplinarian, a hard worker, and a part-time orphan. He was Raised in a semi-related home not really knowing who he was or where he came from and yet having to become who he needed to be. Truth be told we all are part-time orphans in one way or another. Being abandoned by the status quo of expectations of others and finding out who we are intended to be in this thing called life. Yet in the midst of it all, he was a man of his word. Whenever he said he was going to do something he did it. I never had to second guess it. I have always admired that about my dad. He always to the best of his ability kept his word.

I can recall day by day my dad going to work overnight and getting home in the morning carrying 2 gallons of milk and 3 loaves of bread to feed a family of 9. You see when he married my mother, he made a promise to provide for her; therefore, he did. Every night the same thing. The woman that I have become today is because of who my father was to me, and who my mother's father was to me. By them being men, true to their word, helped to shape me and build trust in a father's word. Not only am I sensitive to the words of my natural father but I am in tune with the words of my supernatural Father.

Watching my children grow up I remember if they wanted to do something or needed permission the first thing, I would tell them was, "Go ask your father." These words were ingrained in me from childhood. " GO ASK YOUR FATHER and whatever HE says that's it" somehow the practice of asking my natural father for permission, instruction, opinions, and a plain old hug has formed in me the expectation and more of my heavenly father.

My oldest son Nick is an example of the power of a father's word I had experienced a horrible life-threatening situation where death was on the horizon my husband a strong man of faith had multiple decisions to make in regards how to handle not only what we were going through but how to protect our children and encourage them to know that God our heavenly father always has the last say. One of the first decisions that my husband made was not to tell our children how bad the situation was especially Nick, who was in his second year of college he made that decision because of the detriment and the emotional trauma it would have caused our children and being a good father, you never want to kill your own seed, nor do you ever want to validate your fears.

Well, everyone is not at the same level my nephew reached out to Nick and said Man your mom is really sick you need to get to the hospital and Nick said what are you talking about? My nephew said I'm at the hospital with your mom and she is not doing well the doctors said she is going to die; Nick asked his cousin where is my dad? During that time my husband was enroute to the hospital. Nick told his cousin my dad has not called me, and my dad has not told me anything, so until I hear it from my dad, I'm not going to believe it, end of story.

What is remarkably interesting in this whole scenario is it was very true what my nephew told Nick, but because Nick has such a trust and a connection with the word of his father, even the facts become a lie when it doesn't come from the father. I wonder how many of us have gotten facts about a situation from a reliable source but because it was not what your daddy said it had no credence? How many of us have missed the mark, because we strayed away from the voice of our fathers? How many of us have errors because we did not hear or connect with our father's voice? When you are accustomed to hearing your father's voice you attach your outcome with a sense of assurance knowing that whatever my daddy has said, that so shall it be. Our Father in heaven has said many things to us about us and for us, this is the voice, and these are the words that we should live by, believe, and rely on.

Reflections...

THE LATE BLOOMER
M.U.M.S.

by

MARQUE SHAFFER

DEDICATION

To all those who were given up on or counted out because it looked as if their window had closed. God has a season for the Late Bloomer. To my wife Lisa, daughters Sydney, Aerial, Meagan and Alexi and my parents, Otha and Flora Shaffer, you make life even more worth living.

Marque Shaffer currently pastor's Freedom Fellowship Ministry. He is married to the love of his life, Lisa Shaffer. They have been blessed with four incredible daughters. The focus of Marque's ministry is on individuals obtaining freedom , through faith in God and His Word, from the bondages of life, brought on by sinful choices. Marque has personally been freed from a drug and alcohol addiction for over 25 years and regularly and freely shares his testimony. Marque and Lisa have ministered to countless individuals, couples, and families from their personal story of victory and redemption by God's grace. Many have found salvation, hope and restoration from their experiences.

Contact Information:

Email: lsam95@sbcglobal.net

Story Eight
LATE BLOOMER (M.U.M.S.)

*H*ave you ever felt like it was too late for you or someone you care about to launch in life, to achieve something, to make it, to grow up? Have you given in to the belief that all opportunities have passed you by? Be encouraged, despite how it looks or how you feel. You or the one you care about might just be a **M.U.M.S.**

Not all flowers bloom in the Spring that's why God

made **M.U.M.S.**

My **U**nfinished **M**aturation **S**eason transformed

into **M**aking **U**nfinished **M**oments **S**ucceed

-The Late Bloomer

Each year, as the Summer wanes and Fall approaches, a vibrant array of colors comes on the scene. These colors are different from the changing leaves of the trees. They are rich and varied...purples, yellows, oranges, and lavenders. Bam! Here are chrysanthemums or **M.U.M.S.** for short. It is as if Spring has burst back on the scene; defying the inevitable change of the season to come and its dark, dreary, lifeless spirit. The late arrival of **M.U.M.S.** in the year is symbolic of the hope that exists in the "Fall" season of a person's life. Many people seem to follow the in-seasonal pattern of making something happen early in their lives, like a Spring flower. They enjoy the benefits of a timely and early start in life and the benefits of flowers blooming in season, so to speak. However, many of us miss the moment(s). Our lives were on track for a harvest in-season, but something happened.

Some kind of drought, storm, disease, or sabotage, occurred and ruined our time of blossoming. We and the world around us looked, waited, and wanted, but nothing. What do you do now? Season after season, nothing comes forth. Years, relationships, opportunities, come and go, but what needs to occur in you and through you, lies dormant, hindered, discouraged. Is it an unfortunate set of circumstances totally out of your control that has held your bloom back? Is it your own poor choices and character flaws behaving like a moving and rolling roadblock to your destiny? There is yet hope.

The Bible is replete with late bloomers (in that state for various reasons). Some have not bloomed due to their own choices and others because of what someone else has chosen for them. The resulting consequences held them back. They were runners, reprobate, resistant, rebellious, and more. But God still had a heart and a plan for them (for you). They went about their lives as they saw fit, still, having not come forth into their life's purpose. Then something significant happened, initiating a change of course. This event or set of circumstances stimulated the seed to blossom, although later than expected, right on time for what God intended.

Late Bloomer (The Rebel)
Samson (Judges 13-16)

M.U.M.S. (My Unfinished Maturation Season)
Rebel without a cause.
Rebel with a cause.
Rebel just because you can be, is often what it becomes.

All of your life you have done opposite the norm, you went left when told to go right. You stood up when told to sit down. No reason for it, other than to be contrary, to not conform, to do your own thing. You can't help it that you're strong-willed.

There was a time when being a rebel served you well. Maybe it was not useful during your childhood and teenage years, where it only got you spankings, groundings, and a whole lot of *"me time"*, but later, as you entered a season in your life where rebellion was cool, exhilarating, attractive, and freeing. It allowed you to *"do you"* and no one could stop you. However, for every planting season, a harvest follows. It has been said that "The harvest is always greater than the seed."

Now all those seeds of rebellion are coming to bloom and your life is experiencing a "bumper crop". Of course, you were not expecting such a windfall. It is coming exactly when you have decided to settle in and make something out of your life.

Maybe you finally secured a decent job; one that will afford you the independence you crave and need at this point in your life. You could be a recent graduate, newly divorced, or paroled. Whatever the case, now is the time for moving forward, but...

Years of rebellion and neglecting rules and structure have left you emotionally immature and undisciplined. It shows up on the job, the next job, and the next one. There's a common theme of insubordination and unprofessionalism that follows you, which of course stems from your foundation of disregarding authority and established rules. Perhaps you found the right person and are pursuing a meaningful relationship for the first time in a long time. But it seems that no matter what you do or try to do, eventually, that rebel in you appears. Self-centered ways erode and undermine the "newfound" relationship you were hoping would be long-lasting. You truly want it to work but you can't get out of your own way, because you never really have tried. The person you nurtured, coddled, and cultivated for years now has you, hostage...The Rebel

This may sound like an indictment over something that has always been a part of your makeup, your personality. It's just who you are, how you are wired. Trust me. God knows you. He understands you. He has dealt with Rebels before. It is evident in the life of Samson (*Judges 13-16*).

Samson was the only child of an older couple who thought they couldn't have children. **[Ever thought success couldn't happen for you, only someone else?]** One day an angel of the Lord appeared to Samson's mother and later to his father, Manoah, as well. This son would be special. He would have a miraculous ability, a gift (incredible physical strength). They were given a specific set of rules to govern his diet and grooming. Since this child would have a special assignment from the Lord, they and he needed to follow those rules and adhere to a specific vow, a Nazarite vow. The specifics of that vow were clear {Judges 13} 1) Don't drink wine or strong drink. 2) Don't eat anything unclean, in accordance with Jewish customs. 3) Don't cut hair. Simple! **[What is it about simple instructions that are so hard to follow?]**

But from the time he was of age, Samson, disregarded the norms of the Jewish culture. Like the time he went after a woman of another race, a Philistine; demanding that his parents make a way for him to have her. He eventually got what he wanted, but in the end, it resulted in her death, the death of her father and a thousand Philistine's. In his rebellion, he toyed and played with her people until it ended tragically. **[Has your rebellion caused irreversible harm to others?]** Now when we read the story about this incident (Judges 14, 15), it reveals that God used Samson's rebellion to bring about His own purpose. It was Samson's assignment given before his birth to serve as a judge for the Jewish people and defend them against the Philistines. Yet, it was his rebellion that instigated this encounter. God could and would have done just the same if Samson had obeyed the rules. **[Does the end justify the means just because it worked out in the end? Is the collateral damage done to others justified?]**

Eventually, Samson's strong will and lust for his way of doing things would lead down a path where his gift and his purpose would appear to perish; to go unfulfilled, unfinished, never to bloom. The Rebel, Samson, ran into Delilah (*Judges 16*), another Philistine women. **[Time after time after time of trying the same thing, the same way and expecting different.]** Whatever Delilah had, short-circuited his ability to hold back the secret of the very vow governing his gift and purpose. **[Has rebellion ever caused you to violate or abandon your core beliefs?]** He told her all his heart and even about "never cutting his hair." Before he knew it, he woke up as bald as an eagle and as weak as a blade of grass. This led to Samson being overcome by his enemies, blinded and enslaved; gift gone, purpose lost, and never maturing to what could have been. Season missed! **[What has rebellion stolen from you?]**

His adherence to his rebel nature has sabotaged his life, his mission, and his goals. His parents and many others had most likely given up hope that he would ever amount to anything. "It's too late now." He'll never get it together." "Just face the facts. It wasn't meant to be." "You shouldn't waste your time waiting anymore." These are the statements made by those who had expectations and hopes for Samson (you). It seems like God's plan and purpose for Samson (you) will not be fulfilled.

Just when it looked like it was over, and all hope is lost. Samson's hair began to grow back. Although his eyesight was gone, he had a laser focus now on whom he was and his life's purpose as designed by the Father, God. Before his life's journey ended, he enlisted some help **[As we all need to get on track]** from a young fellow and was able to position himself, to defeat the enemy of God and his people, in one final act of obedience. Now, behind a simple haircut, Samson was no longer a Rebel, but a **M.U.M.S.** (**M**aking **U**nfinished **M**oments **S**ucceed); righteously blossoming for the Lord.

The Bible tells us in *Philippians 1:6* "I am certain that God, who began a good work within you, will continue his work until it is finally finished on the day when Christ Jesus returns - NLT". Simply stated, "What God has started, He will finish."

What will it take for you to come forth, Rebel, Late Bloomer? For Samson it started with a haircut, which turned out to be the turning point in his life. Maybe it's already happening in yours. It could be staring at you from the mirror, a family member or friend, a circumstance or consequence. You will know it when it happens and I promise you it will be because the God of all creation, the Giver and Sustainer of life, loves you and wants you to bloom. He has ordained a season for you that circumstances, situations, persons, or things, cannot deny.

If you are not sure how He is intervening in your life, try surrendering your will to His by simply starting with a prayer like this: "Father God forgive me for my rebellion. Please lead me into the path you created for me. I believe you can. I believe you love me. I believe you sent Jesus to die for me and to save me. I want to bloom for you."

Reflections...

ADAPT AND OVERCOME

by

DR. ROBERT L. WATTS, JR.

DEDICATION

I dedicate this to all of you who choose to stand in faith on God's Word amid adverse situations. Keep being an encouragement to others through your testimony, as you see God's faithfulness operate in your life. Ephesian 6:13-15, *"13 Therefore take up the whole armor of God, that you may be able to withstand in the evil day, and having done all, to stand.*

14 Stand therefore, having girded your waist with truth, having put on the breastplate of righteousness, 15 and having shod your feet with the preparation of the gospel of peace;..."

Dr. Robert L. Watts, Jr. is an engaging teacher and speaker. Robert (aslo referred to as Dr. Rob) has been in ministry for over thirty plus years, teaching, training, and empowering others through the refreshing messages as he delivers with perspective, relevancy, inspiration, and a touch of humor. He and his wife are founders of One Flesh Ministries, Inc. a 501c3. He has authored several other books, conducts workshops and seminars to empower others, and helps aspiring writers to become published authors. For over 30 years, he's served in various capacities of ministerial and professional leadership, while training and building other future leaders in the process. His passion to help equip people in ministry lead him to developing www.ofmbi.com, an educational division of One Flesh Ministries., Inc.

Through his educational and training pursuits he's earned several degrees and certifications. He holds a doctorate in Ministry and working on the completion of his doctorate in Business Administration. He has a true passion to help others discover & achieve their God-given purpose.

Contact Information:

Email: drrob@drrobempowerment.com
Web: www.drrobempowerment.com
Twitter: @mentalmotive40
Instagram: @drrob_

Story Nine
ADAPT AND OVERCOME

What a blessing it was to help bring this divine project together. It was my honor to compile and publish this great historic literary work. Engaging with each of the contributing authors with what they individually brought to this book project has been rewarding in itself; and I believe it will be rewarding for everyone who reads it. Their stories from the heart ministered to me, giving me a new level of appreciation and respect for each of them.

Some of the authors shared excerpts from future solo book project that will be revealed in due time. So be on the lookout for more amazing things to come. Naturally, like with most productive things, obstacles tried to hinder the process of producing this book. Some might expect this when dealing with multiple authors on a single project. On a spiritual note, discernment is crucial when you're doing a divine assignment to recognize when the adversary will try to bring about delays and detours.

All the contributing authors are on one accord in believing this book will be a blessing to the masses. Although we see in part now, we have faith God will reveal the greater that shall come. Each author kept pressing forward to share what was laid on their hearts. As you have read, some of the stories were very personable and somewhat vulnerable for the authors. But all of us knew that our TESTS bring TESTimonies that need to be shared.

I want to encourage you to always keep pressing even amid obstacles. Most of the time, the true inner strength is found when you push yourself past your mental boundaries and assumed fears. I had a former co-worker that would always make the statement, 'Adapt and overcome.' This meant, regardless of the obstacle(s), we can still find a way to adjust and find a work-around to ensure the mission was accomplished. The phrase was something she caught from her Marine Corp husband. The statement also included dealing with one's personal thoughts, emotions, and reactions to adverse situations.

When I think of the statement, I'm reminded of some

years ago. I had a legal suit against me, which was a first for me. Honestly, the experience was intimidating. Having legal papers delivered to my job and residence and attorneys constantly harassing, became a bit much to process. To my surprise, I also had a wage garnishment submitted to my employer, which brought on more embarrassment and concerns. It felt like I was caught in a sudden downward spiral happening all at once, without any branches to grab onto as I was falling. I couldn't afford for my wages to be garnished; I had basic bills to try and pay to take care of the basics for me and my family, like food-shelter, etc. But the other side didn't care about that, this wasn't personal-it was just business as usual for them.

My first time I was required to show up in court, as required to respond to the lawsuit, was memorable. Walking into the County Court building automatically brought upon the sense of the unknown and heightened heartbeats. After everyone goes through the security lines, like the airport, I found my way to hallway of elevators to figure out the floor where the courtroom would be for the case against me. The elevators seemed to be filled with two types of people, suited up lawyers and concerned patron trying to figure out what to do in their undesirable situations. The hallways seem like something out of a Stephen King film with long, dim, and everyone appeared to walk like Matrix or Zombie characters.

I didn't know what to expect when I walked into the courtroom filled with people. I didn't know everyone's business was out in the open as their cases were called before the judge. I didn't know what I was supposed to say. Not knowing feels powerless and opens the door for fear. When fear settles in, one easily succumbs to whatever the adversary (opponent) throws at you. I just felt like a sitting duck. As my case was called by the bailiff, the case of (institution) vs. Robert Watts. 'Phew' deep breath, I approach the bench and I don't recall what was said by the judge and the institutions attorney.

Fortunately, my first court appearance was to acknowledge the suit, the wage garnishment, and a new date set for follow up. So, after getting directives by the judge and exiting the courtroom in such disappointment, the attorney representing the institution did have to go over some paperwork with me. We exited the courtroom and sat down on one of the hallway benches. And she, the attorney, did something I truly appreciated-she asked how I was doing. I was honest on how I felt and the stress this has brought on for me and my family. She advised me of something that was very logical, which was to try and not to let this stress me, **it is not worth it**. Although, it was easy for her to say, but I could tell she was sincere; her words helped snapped me out of a self-pity zone.

After going over the small talk with the attorney, there was paperwork I still had to submit at another department on another floor; and after submitting to that department, I had to get papers stamped on another floor. It was like a confusing human maze. I will never forget as I was standing in line along with the other concerned faces in the same boat of legal challenges, there was a man, approximately in his late 20s, early thirties. He was at the front of the line to submit his papers. Suddenly, he fell onto the ground into a seizure. It was heart-breaking because I knew (and blurted out) "it's because of all the stress dealing with these lawsuits." No offense to County workers, but for some of them-it's a regular day on the job and their level of compassion seemed waxed-cold. The security came to assist, but his seizure stopped before medics were needed. After seeing that, I was determined not to allow anxiety-fear-worry, about this situation, get the best of me.

Conveniently, the courthouse was down the street from my job. When I returned to my office, I had to just sit and take a moment to woo-sah. At that point, I decided to pray differently. Not pray an 'Oh, help me God', but a prayer of, 'God show me how to equip myself.' I made the decision not to think in a victim mindset. I had to, 'Adapt and overcome.' I wasn't just going to roll over and allow the unknown to triumph over me. The end may not turn out as I prefer, but I won't go out without standing my ground and being as equipped as possible. Over the next few days, I started to pray and research, and in my search, I discovered that I did have an option to protect my finances up to a certain amount. Fortunately, the amount was high enough that covered my wages! I suddenly began to fill this surge of empowerment.

After discovering what paperwork, I needed to file to enact this stay against the wage garnishment, I scheduled to go down to the courthouse and be ready for my next appoint before the judge. When the time came for the court appointment, I felt different this time. I didn't have same timidity and ignorance as before. I was better informed, more confident, less stressed, and knew some truth of my rights. As I stood before the judge next to their attorney and presented my paperwork to stop the garnishments-the judge looked at the attorney and said, "he's right." Judgment was made in my favor. The feeling of a small, sweet victory was one I won't forget. I learned a valuable lesson, and that is not to dwell in Victimville. We must make efforts to empower ourselves with as much faith and truth about any situation that is opposing against you in order to strategize on how to approach it.

It is the same spiritually, equip yourself with God's Word and prayer. It's the only way to know your spiritual-legal standing against our adversary, the devil. The devil is always before God trying to throw spiritual lawsuits against us because of our short-coming (Revelation 12:10). He can win on many occasions because of his dependence on our succumbing to the intimidation of how big obstacles may appear and our ignorance. But just as Jesus did in The Wilderness (Matthew 4: 1-11), we too must do, and that is to speak The Word of God in faith and authority. We have two options to reside in, Victimville or Victoryville-the choice is ours to make. Remember, God gives us options that will work out for our good (Romans 8:28).

This Collaborative Project is truly one of the highlights of my past book publishing projects. The root word, collaborate is defined as working jointly on an activity; especially to produce or create something. We are all proud to have worked together in creating this divine assignment so that it will be an impartation in the lives of all that read and hear about it. May the abundance of God's blessings rain heavily in your life.

Dr. Rob

Reflections...

Isaiah 45:8

8 "You heavens above, rain down my righteousness; let the clouds shower it down. Let the earth open wide, let salvation spring up, let righteousness flourish with it; I, the LORD, have created it.

www.ingramcontent.com/pod-product-compliance
Lightning Source LLC
LaVergne TN
LVHW021351080426
835508LV00020B/2227